DESPERATION SPEAKS

JOHN SMITHWICK

DESPERATION SPEAKS
ISBN 9780615505244
COPYRIGHT © 2011 BY JOHN SMITHWICK MINISTRIES INTERNATIONAL (JSMI)
P.O. BOX 1860
CATOOSA, OK 74015

PRINTED IN CANADA

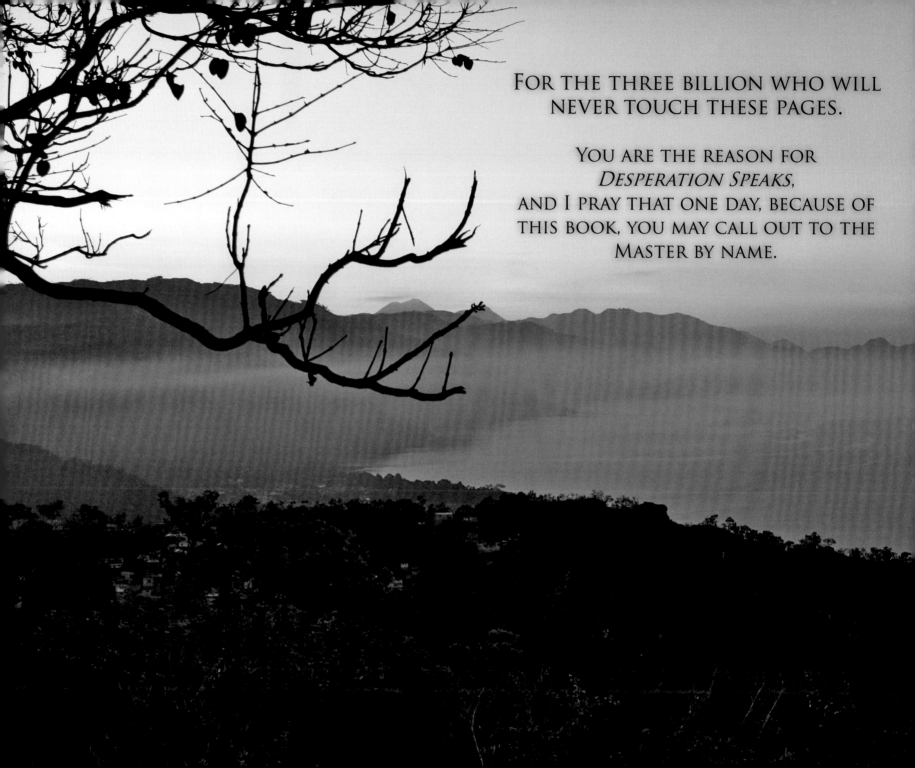

FOR THE THREE BILLION WHO WILL
NEVER TOUCH THESE PAGES.

YOU ARE THE REASON FOR
DESPERATION SPEAKS,
AND I PRAY THAT ONE DAY, BECAUSE OF
THIS BOOK, YOU MAY CALL OUT TO THE
MASTER BY NAME.

The pictures that appear in *Desperation Speaks* were captured by selected team members of John Smithwick Ministries International a.k.a. Global Ventures.

The following pages contain photos taken from the years of 2008 through 2011 in the countries of Cambodia, Guatemala, Haiti, Nepal, Peru, the Philippines, South Africa, and Thailand. The stories of these nations, these faces, have gripped the hearts of team members everywhere.

As Global Ventures ministers in countless lost and overlooked nations, the cries of the precious people compel us to share their stories and etch their beautiful faces into the hearts of the rest of the world.

The heartbeat of God pulses throughout the seams of this book, and those who listen shamelessly, openly, and honestly will hear it, feel it, and find it.

John Smithwick

"LISTEN TO MY CRY,
FOR I AM IN DESPERATE
NEED; RESCUE ME FROM
THOSE WHO PURSUE
ME, FOR THEY ARE TOO
STRONG FOR ME. SET ME
FREE FROM MY PRISON,
THAT I MAY PRAISE YOUR
NAME."

PSALM 142:6&7

"EVERYTHING ON
EARTH CHANGES
AND PASSES AWAY,

EXCEPT FOR WHAT IS
ETERNAL.

THE ONLY THINGS
THAT ARE ETERNAL
ARE THE SOULS OF
MANKIND."

JERRY O'DELL

"OUR GOD OF GRACE OFTEN GIVES US A SECOND CHANCE, BUT THERE IS NO SECOND CHANCE TO HARVEST A RIPE CROP."

KURT VON SCHLEICHER

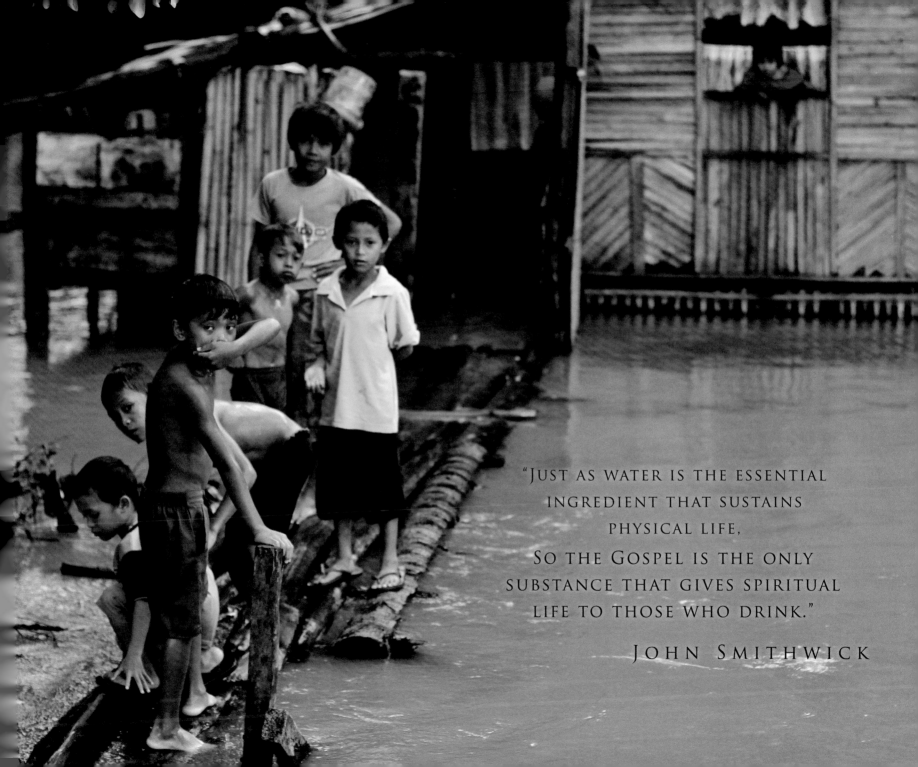

"JUST AS WATER IS THE ESSENTIAL
INGREDIENT THAT SUSTAINS
PHYSICAL LIFE,
SO THE GOSPEL IS THE ONLY
SUBSTANCE THAT GIVES SPIRITUAL
LIFE TO THOSE WHO DRINK."

JOHN SMITHWICK

"THE GOSPEL IS ONLY GOOD NEWS IF IT GETS THERE IN TIME."

CARL F. H. HENRY

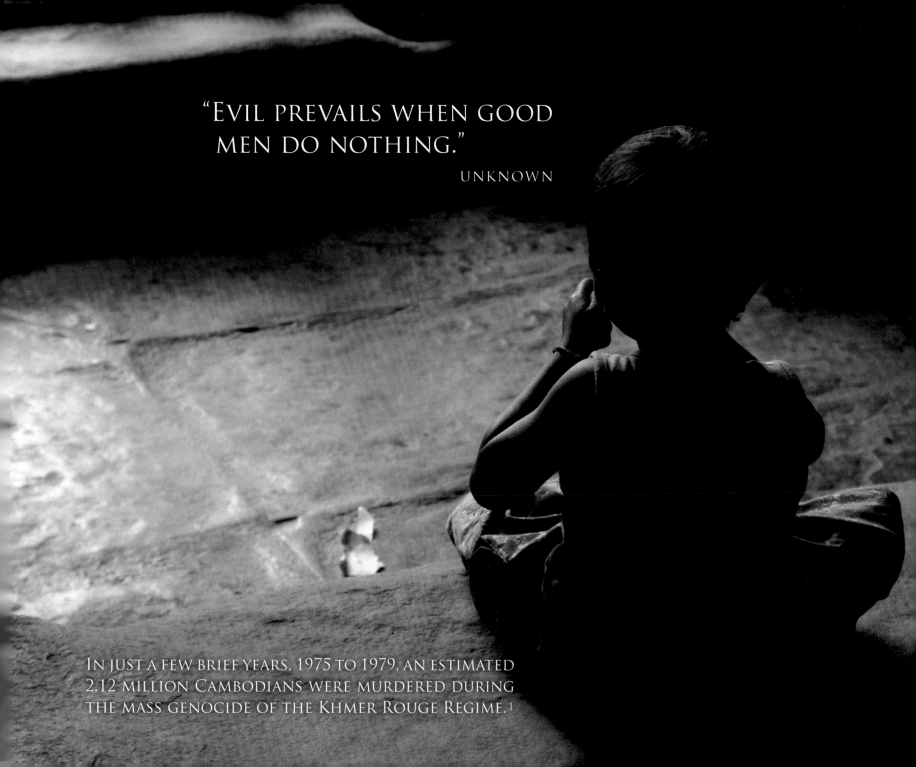

"EVIL PREVAILS WHEN GOOD
MEN DO NOTHING."

UNKNOWN

IN JUST A FEW BRIEF YEARS, 1975 TO 1979, AN ESTIMATED
2.12 MILLION CAMBODIANS WERE MURDERED DURING
THE MASS GENOCIDE OF THE KHMER ROUGE REGIME.[1]

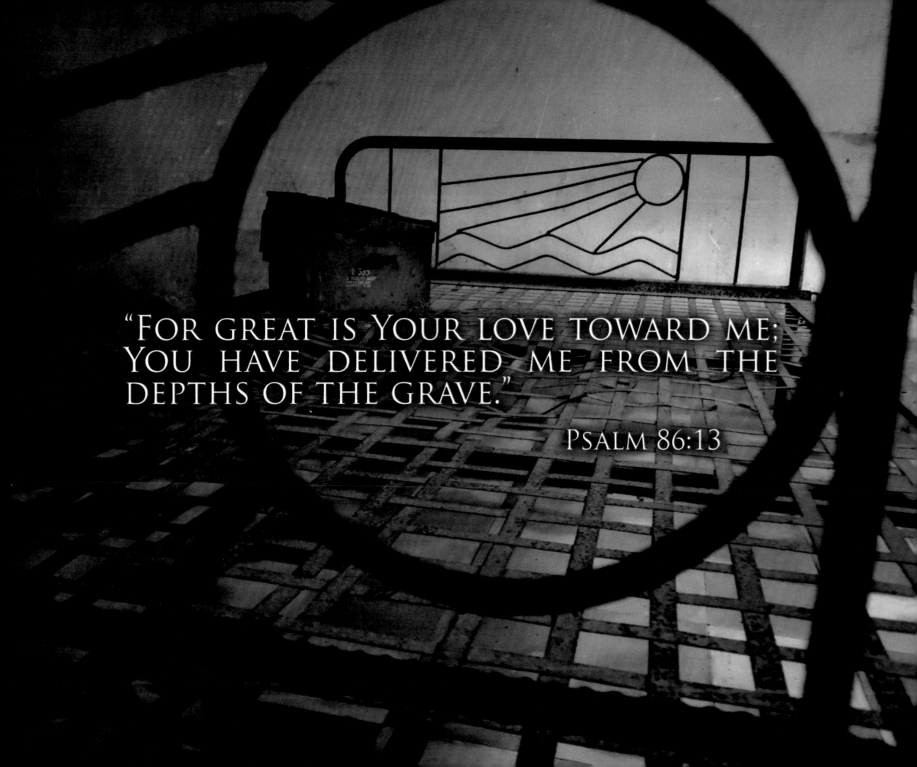

"For great is Your love toward me;
You have delivered me from the
depths of the grave."

Psalm 86:13

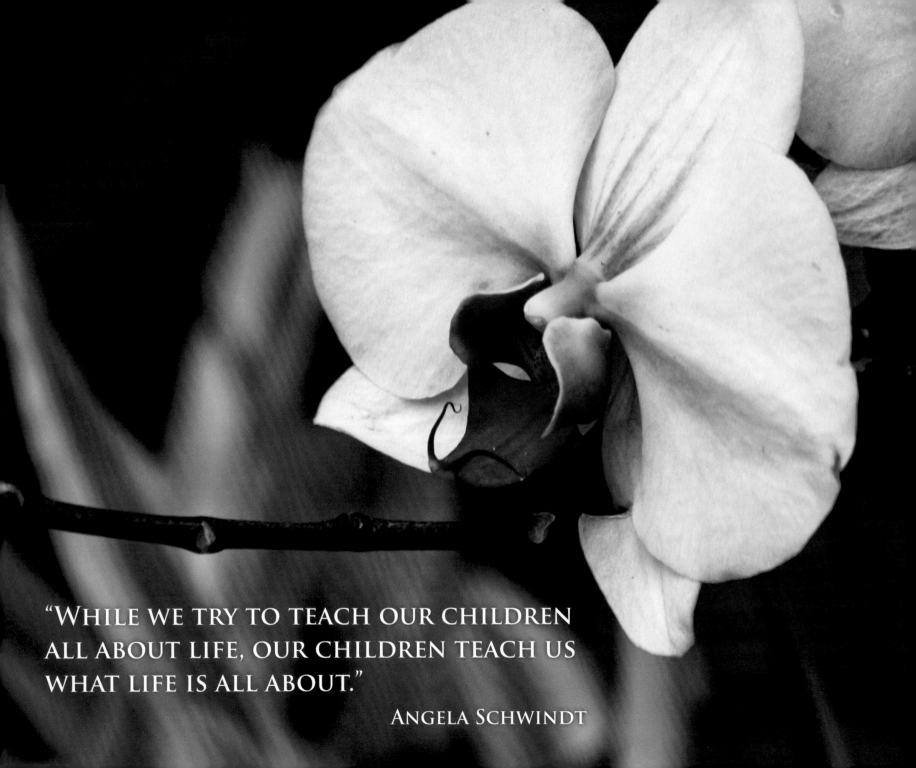

"While we try to teach our children all about life, our children teach us what life is all about."

Angela Schwindt

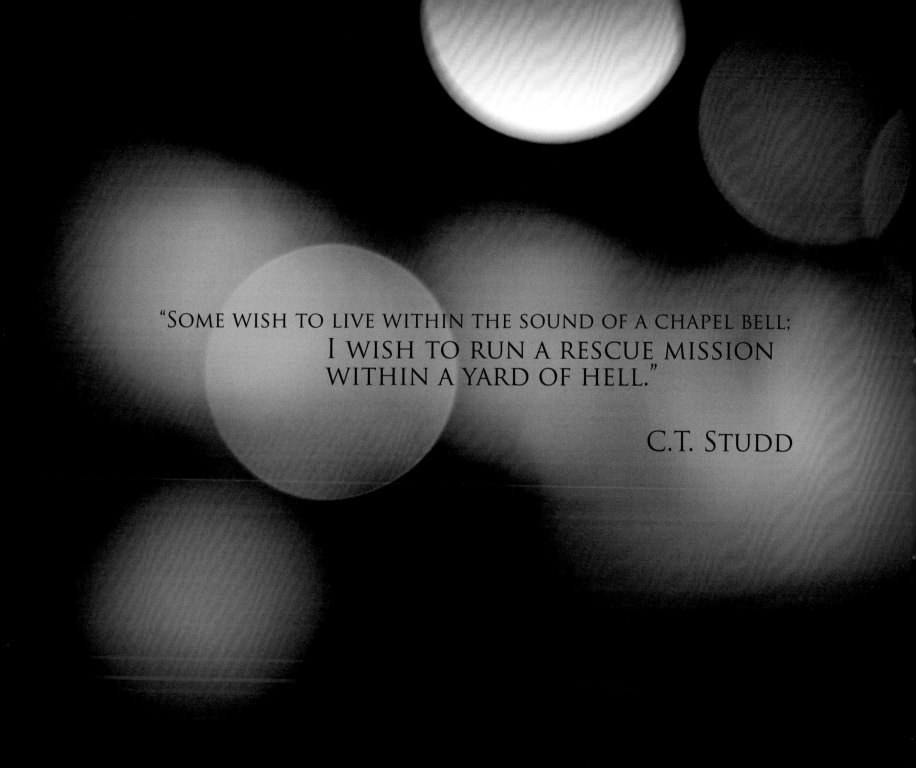

"SOME WISH TO LIVE WITHIN THE SOUND OF A CHAPEL BELL;
I WISH TO RUN A RESCUE MISSION
WITHIN A YARD OF HELL."

C.T. STUDD

IN THE PAST 30 YEARS, OVER 30 MILLION WOMEN AND CHILDREN HAVE BEEN TRAFFICKED FOR SEXUAL EXPLOITATION IN ASIA ALONE.[2]

"I HAVE BUT ONE CANDLE OF LIFE TO BURN, AND I WOULD RATHER BURN IT OUT IN A LAND FILLED WITH DARKNESS THAN IN A LAND FLOODED WITH LIGHT."

JOHN KEITH FALCONER

"This Generation of Christians is responsible for this generation of souls on the earth."
Keith Green

"NO ONE HAS THE RIGHT TO HEAR THE GOSPEL TWICE, WHILE THERE REMAINS SOMEONE WHO HAS NOT HEARD IT ONCE."

OSWALD J. SMITH

"DESPERATION SPEAKS OF WHAT A PERSON NEEDS THE MOST AT ANY GIVEN MOMENT.

AT EVERY GIVEN MOMENT, A PERSON'S GREATEST NEED IS SALVATION."

JOHN SMITHWICK

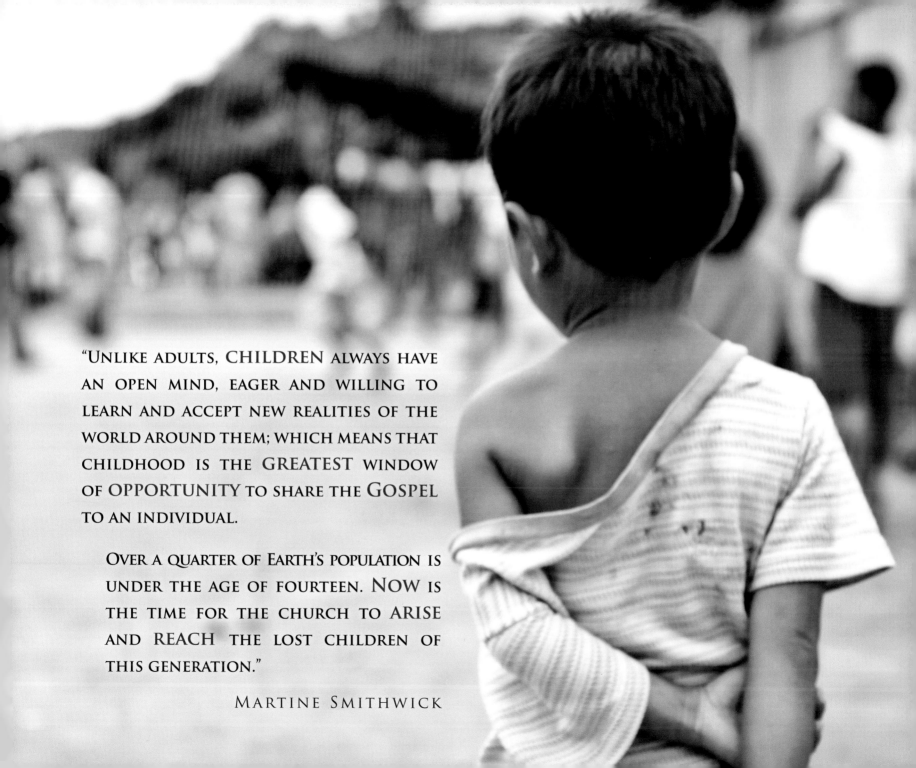

"UNLIKE ADULTS, CHILDREN ALWAYS HAVE AN OPEN MIND, EAGER AND WILLING TO LEARN AND ACCEPT NEW REALITIES OF THE WORLD AROUND THEM; WHICH MEANS THAT CHILDHOOD IS THE GREATEST WINDOW OF OPPORTUNITY TO SHARE THE GOSPEL TO AN INDIVIDUAL.

OVER A QUARTER OF EARTH'S POPULATION IS UNDER THE AGE OF FOURTEEN. NOW IS THE TIME FOR THE CHURCH TO ARISE AND REACH THE LOST CHILDREN OF THIS GENERATION."

MARTINE SMITHWICK

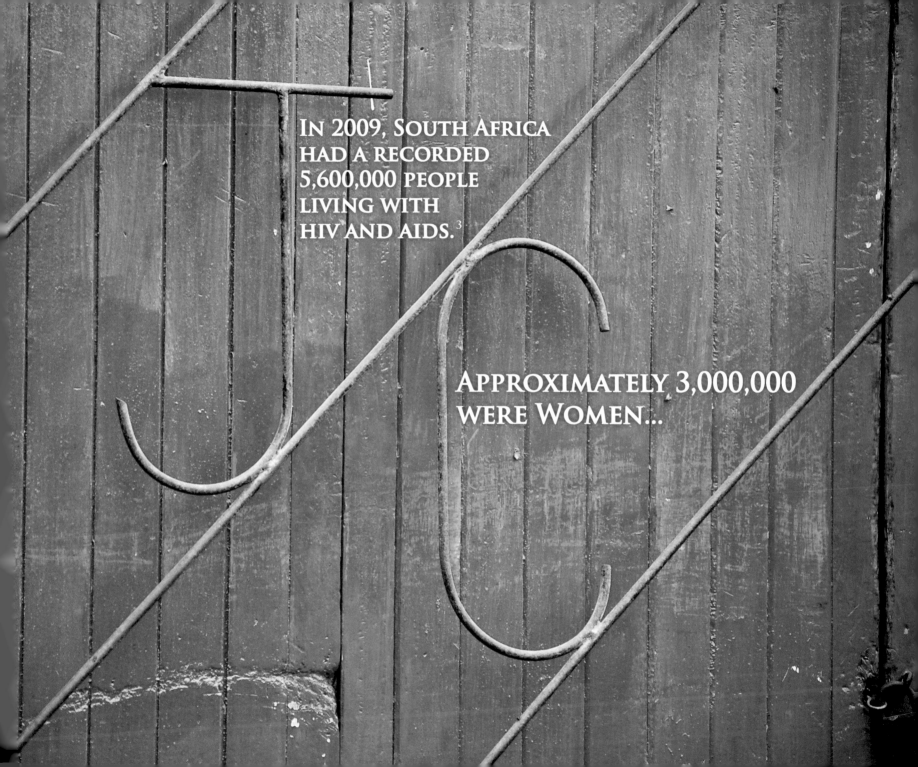

In 2009, South Africa had a recorded 5,600,000 people living with HIV and AIDS.[3]

Approximately 3,000,000 were Women...

"MY SALVATION AND MY HONOR DEPEND ON
GOD; HE IS MY MIGHTY ROCK, MY REFUGE."

PSALM 62:7

"I HAVE BUT ONE PASSION - IT IS HE, IT IS HE ALONE...

THE WORLD IS THE FIELD AND THE FIELD IS THE WORLD; AND HENCEFORTH, THAT COUNTRY SHALL BE MY HOME...

WHERE I CAN BE MOST USED IN WINNING SOULS FOR CHRIST."

LUDWIG VON ZINZENDORF

"WE TALK OF THE SECOND COMING WHEN HALF OF THE WORLD HAS NEVER HEARD OF THE FIRST."

OSWALD J. SMITH

"THE MOST EVIL THING ON THE EARTH IS WHEN THE GOSPEL IS WITHHELD FROM PEOPLE WHO HAVE NEVER HEARD IT."

JERRY O'DELL

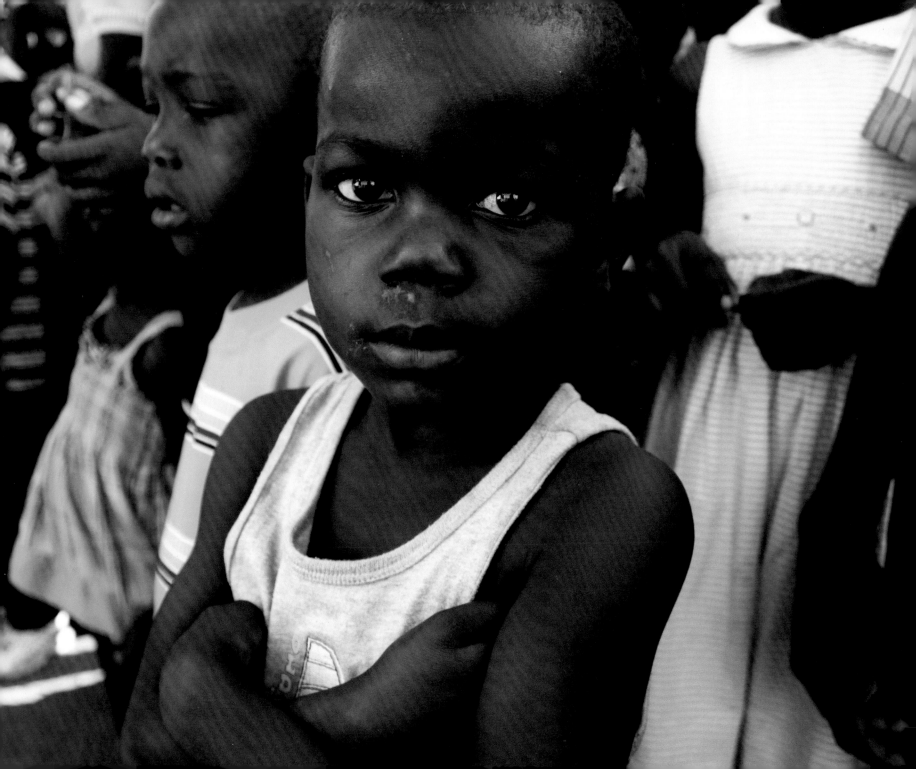

"True STRENGTH lies in SUBMISSION, which permits one to dedicate his life through DEVOTION, to something beyond himself."

Henry Miller

"HOW BEAUTIFUL ARE THE FEET OF THOSE WHO BRING GOOD NEWS."

Romans 10:15

"THEREFORE, WHOEVER HUMBLES HIMSELF LIKE THIS CHILD IS THE GREATEST IN THE KINGDOM OF HEAVEN."

MATTHEW 18:4

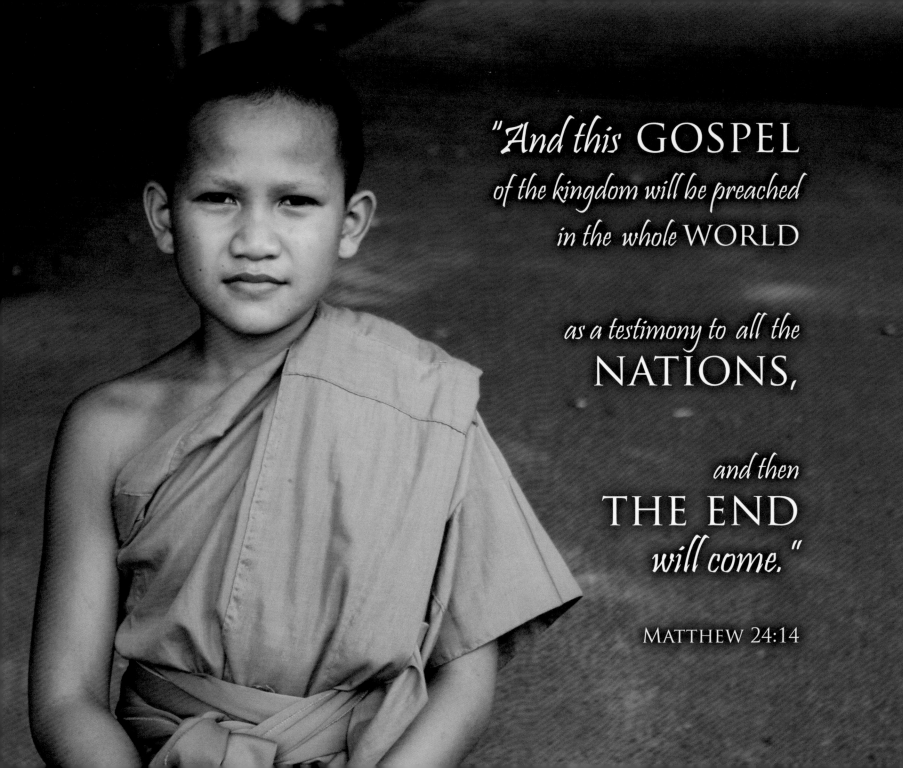

"And this GOSPEL of the kingdom will be preached in the whole WORLD

as a testimony to all the NATIONS,

and then THE END will come."

MATTHEW 24:14

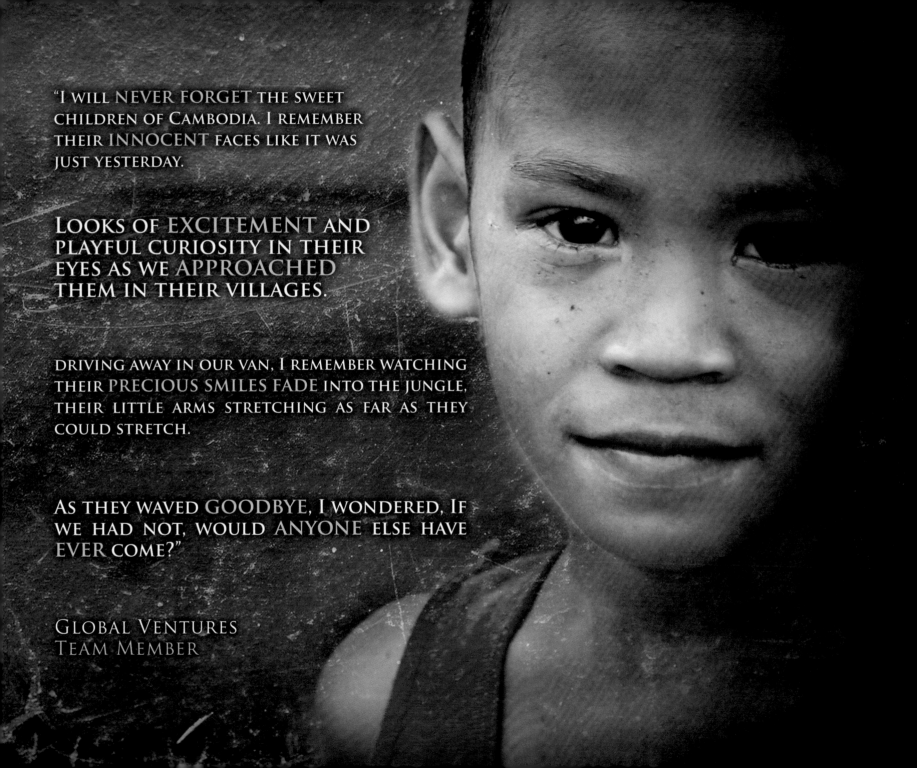

"I WILL NEVER FORGET THE SWEET CHILDREN OF CAMBODIA. I REMEMBER THEIR INNOCENT FACES LIKE IT WAS JUST YESTERDAY.

LOOKS OF EXCITEMENT AND PLAYFUL CURIOSITY IN THEIR EYES AS WE APPROACHED THEM IN THEIR VILLAGES.

DRIVING AWAY IN OUR VAN, I REMEMBER WATCHING THEIR PRECIOUS SMILES FADE INTO THE JUNGLE, THEIR LITTLE ARMS STRETCHING AS FAR AS THEY COULD STRETCH.

AS THEY WAVED GOODBYE, I WONDERED, IF WE HAD NOT, WOULD ANYONE ELSE HAVE EVER COME?"

GLOBAL VENTURES
TEAM MEMBER

3,000,000,000
HAVE NEVER HEARD
THE GOSPEL ONE TIME.

2,000,000,000
HAVE NO ACCESS TO IT.[4]

THE MOST UNREACHED AREA OF THE WORLD IS IN THE 10/40 WINDOW (APPROXIMATELY 10 DEGREES TO 40 DEGREES NORTH LATITUDE) INCLUDING NORTHERN AFRICA, THE MIDDLE EAST, ASIA, AND ANY COUNTRY THAT HAS AT LEAST 50 PERCENT OF ITS LANDMASS WITHIN THOSE SAME BOUNDARIES.

COUNTRIES IN THE 10/40 WINDOW: [4]

AFGHANISTAN	BURKINA FASO	ERITREA	ISRAEL
ALBANIA	CAMBODIA	ETHIOPIA	JAPAN
ALGERIA	CHAD	GAMBIA	JORDAN
AZERBAIJAN	CHINA	GUINEA	KAZAKHSTAN
BAHRAIN	CHINA, HONG KONG	GUINEA-BISSAU	KOREA, NORTH
BANGLADESH	CHINA, MACAU	INDIA	KUWAIT
BENIN	DJIBOUTI	INDONESIA	KYRGYZSTAN
BHUTAN	EAST TIMOR	IRAN	LAOS
BRUNEI	EGYPT	IRAQ	LEBANON
LIBYA	NIGER	SUDAN	UZBEKISTAN
MALAYSIA	NIGERIA	SYRIA	VIETNAM
MALDIVES	OMAN	TAIWAN	WEST BANK / GAZA
MALI	PAKISTAN	TAJIKISTAN	WESTERN SAHARA
MAURITANIA	QATAR	THAILAND	YEMEN
MONGOLIA	SAUDI ARABIA	TUNISIA	
MOROCCO	SENEGAL	TURKEY	
MYANMAR (BURMA)	SOMALIA	TURKMENISTAN	
NEPAL	SRI LANKA	UNITED ARAB EMIRATES	

GLOBAL VENTURES

THE DESPERATE CRIES OF THE LOST PEOPLE OF THE EARTH RING IN THE HEART AND SOUL OF GLOBAL VENTURES. THE BURNING DESIRE TO REACH OUT AND IMPACT THOSE FORGOTTEN NATIONS HAS MANIFESTED A MYRIAD OF MASS CRUSADES, LEADING TO THE SALVATION OF OVER ONE MILLION SOULS.

EVERY YEAR, JSMI GLOBAL VENTURES TAKES HUNDREDS OF PEOPLE FROM ACROSS AMERICA, CANADA, AND EUROPE TO UNREACHED AREAS OF THE WORLD. GLOBAL VENTURES TEAM TRIPS ARE RADICALLY CHANGING NATIONS THROUGH STRATEGIC EVANGELISM AND CRUSADES, ONE REGION AT A TIME. ON THE STREETS OF FOREIGN NATIONS, MIRACLES FLOW THROUGH THE HANDS OF THE TEAM MEMBERS AS BLIND EYES SEE, DEAF EARS HEAR, AND THOUSANDS EXPERIENCE THE GOSPEL OF CHRIST FOR THE FIRST TIME.

AS THE TEAM MEMBERS WITNESS THE INSPIRING HEALINGS AND SALVATIONS OF THE UNREACHED THROUGH THEIR VOICE, THEY THEMSELVES ARE TRANSFORMED AND FOREVER INFUSED WITH A COMPELLING DESIRE TO REACH THE WORLD. GLOBAL VENTURES FEELS RESPONSIBLE TO AWAKEN OTHERS TO THIS PASSION.

VISIT OUR WEBSITE TO JOIN GLOBAL VENTURES ON A TEAM TRIP, TO PARTNER WITH JSMI IN SAVING THE LOST, AND TO RECEIVE A FREE BROCHURE ABOUT THE HARVEST MISSION.

WWW.GLOBALVENTURES.TV

ACKNOWLEDGEMENTS

THIS BOOK WAS NOT A SINGULAR EFFORT; NOR DID IT APPEAR OVERNIGHT. THROUGH THE HARD WORK OF OUR DEDICATED TEAM THOUGH, IT IS HERE. SO THANK YOU...

TO MY WIFE, MARTINE SMITHWICK, FOR BEING THE MOST INCREDIBLE PARTNER IN LIFE, MINISTRY, AND THIS QUEST FOR SOULS,

TO MY MOTHER, JUNE SMITHWICK, FOR ASSISTING IN THE FINAL EDITING,

TO JOSH QUERIN AND LIZ UZZEL, FOR SPENDING COUNTLESS HOURS EDITING,

TO HOLLY BUTTON, ERIN CAMPBELL, BLAKE RAYMOND, JAMIE LYNN SIVAK, AND WILL WINSLETT, FOR CAPTURING THE INSPIRING PHOTOGRAPHY OF DESPERATION SPEAKS,

AND TO GLOBAL VENTURES TEAM MEMBERS EVERYWHERE, FOR MAKING THE SALVATION OF OVER A MILLION POSSIBLE.

BIBLIOGRAPHY

JOHN SMITHWICK MINISTRIES INTERNATIONAL IS GRATEFUL TO THE INDIVIDUALS AND ORGANIZATIONS FOR THE PERMISSION TO REPRODUCE COPYRIGHTED MATERIAL WITHIN THE PAGES OF THIS BOOK. TO EVERYONE WHO GRANTED OUR REQUESTS, THANK YOU.

ANGELA SCHWINDT: PERMISSION FROM ANGELA SCHWINDT. © 2010 ANGELA SCHWINDT.

HENRY MILLER: FROM *THE TIME OF THE ASSASSINS*, BY HENRY MILLER. © 1956 BY NEW DIRECTIONS PUBLISHING CORP. REPRINTED BY PERMISSION OF NEW DIRECTIONS PUBLISHING.

JERRY O'DELL: FROM *THE MOST EVIL THING ON EARTH* BY JERRY O'DELL. © 2010 JERRY O'DELL.

KEITH GREEN: FROM NO COMPROMISE: *THE LIFE STORY OF KEITH GREEN* BY MELODY GREEN AND DAVID HAZARD. REPRINTED BY THOMAS NELSON PUBLISHERS. © 1989, 2008 MELODY GREEN.

OSWALD J. SMITH: PERMISSION FROM OPERATION MOBILIZATION. © 1986 OPERATION MOBILIZATION.

REFERENCES

1. *COUNTING HELL: THE DEATH TOLL OF THE KHMER ROUGE REGIME IN CAMBODIA.* MEKONG, 2008. WEB. JUN. 2011.

2. "GENERAL ASSEMBLY: TWENTY-SEVENTH SPECIAL SESSION." *UNITED NATIONS: SPECIAL SESSION ON CHILDREN* (2002): 68. *UNICEF.* WEB. JUN. 2011.

3. *GLOBAL REPORT: UNAIDS REPORT ON THE GLOBAL AIDS EPIDEMIC 2010.* UNAIDS. 2010. WEB. JUN. 2011.

4. JOSHUA PROJECT. N.D. WEB. JUN. 2011.

John Smithwick has conducted mass crusades and evangelism outreaches in over 25 countries, bringing the simple Gospel to the unreached and witnessing God perform countless miracles.

Since he founded John Smithwick Ministries International (JSMI) in 1998, John has brought thousands to foreign nations to minister the Gospel as well.

If this book has touched your heart, or to order additional copies, visit our website:

WWW.DesperationSpeaks.com

For additional information about JSMI or Global Ventures, visit our website:

WWW.GLOBALVENTURES.TV

John Smithwick Ministries International
PO Box 1860
Catoosa, OK 74015
info@johnsmithwick.com
info@globalventures.tv

Stay tuned for future books by John Smithwick:

WWW.TWITTER.COM/JohnRSmithwick

...a dar las nuevas a los discípulos,

9 he aquí, Jesús les salió al encuentro, diciendo: ¡Salve! Y ellas, acercándose, abrazaron sus pies, y le adoraron.

10 Entonces Jesús les dijo: No temáis; id, dad las nuevas a mis hermanos, para que vayan a Galilea, y allí me verán.

11 Mientras ellas iban, he aquí unos de la guardia fueron a la ciudad, y dieron aviso a los principales sacerdotes de todas las cosas que habían acontecido.

12 Y reunidos con los ancianos, y habido consejo, dieron...

...suadiremos, y os pondremos a salvo.

15 Y ellos, tomando el dinero, hicieron como se les había instruido. Este dicho se ha divulgado entre los judíos hasta el día de hoy.

16 Pero los once discípulos se fueron a Galilea, al monte donde Jesús les había ordenado.

17 Y cuando le vieron, le adoraron; pero algunos dudaban.

18 Y Jesús se acercó y les habló diciendo: Toda potestad me es dada en el cielo y en la tierra.

19 Por tanto, id, y haced discípulos a todas las naciones, bautizándolos en el nombre del Padre, y del Hijo, y del Espíritu Santo;

20 enseñándoles que guarden todas las cosas que os he mandado; y he aquí yo estoy con vosotros todos los días, hasta el fin del mundo. Amén.

EL SANTO EVANGELIO SEGÚN SAN MARCOS

CAPÍTULO 1

PRINCIPIO del evangelio de Jesucristo, Hijo de Dios.

2 Como está escrito en Isaías el profeta: He aquí yo envío mi mensajero delante de tu faz, el cual preparará tu camino delante de ti.

3 Voz del que clama en el desierto: Preparad el camino del Señor; enderezad sus sendas.

4 Bautizaba Juan en el desierto, y predicaba el bautismo de arrepentimiento para perdón de pecados.

5 Y salían a él toda la provincia de Judea, y todos los de Jerusalén; y eran bautizados por él en el río Jordán, confesando sus pecados.

6 Y Juan estaba vestido de pelo de camello, y tenía un cinto de cuero alrededor de sus lomos; y comía langostas y miel silvestre.

7 Y predicaba, diciendo: Viene tras mí el que es más poderoso que yo, a quien no soy digno de desatar encorvado la correa de su calzado.

8 Yo a la verdad os he bautizado con agua; pero

él os... tu San...

9 Ac... días, q... zaret d... tizado... dán.

10 Y l... del agu... cielos, y... paloma... sobre él.

11 Y vir... cielos que... mi Hijo a... complacen...

12 Y lue... impulsó al...

13 Y estu... sierto cuare... tentado por... taba con l... ángeles le...

14 Desp... encarcela... Galilea... evangelio... Dios,

15 diciendo:... ha cumplido... Dios se ha... pentíos, y... evangelio...

16 Anda... de Galilea,... Andrés su... echaban la r... porque eran pesca...

17 Y les dijo Je...